TORTURE
AND THE
ROMAN INQUISITION

KENNETH GAMBIN

PHOTOGRAPHY
DANIEL CILIA

HERITAGE BOOKS

IN ASSOCIATION WITH
H Heritage Malta
2004

The coat-of-arms of the Roman Inquisition

Insight Heritage Guides Series No: 9
General Editor: Louis J. Scerri

Published by Heritage Books, a subsidiary of
Midsea Books Ltd, Carmelites Street,
Sta Venera HMR 11, Malta
sales@midseabooks.com

*Insight Heritage Guides is a series of books intended
to give an insight into aspects and sites of Malta's
rich heritage, culture and traditions.*

Produced by Mizzi Design & Graphic Services
Printed by Gutenberg Press

Editorial © Heritage Books
Literary © Kenneth Gambin
Photography © Daniel Cilia
except those on pages 5, 8, 9, 12, 13 bottom,
14, and 15 bottom

First published 2004

ISBN: 99932-39-98-4

INTRODUCTION

In the popular imagination the word Inquisition is synonymous with the most horrible tortures. Yet the reality is much different from what any popular fictitious history might suggest. Many of the myths related to the terrible Inquisition that circulated in Europe can be traced back to the late eighteenth and nineteenth century, as part of the secularization process of building up public support and pressure to eliminate clerical privilege and authority over lay people.[1] Lack of knowledge has led to extreme reactions ranging from outright condemnations to hasty rehabilitations of this institution surrounded with an aura of mystery. Although torture was far from being a pleasant experience (and cannot be justified), the scenes of incredible sufferings and the myths of inquisitorial sadism invented by popular writers have little basis in reality, at least where the Roman Inquisition is concerned.

Torture, or the *rigoroso esame*, was indeed used by the Roman Inquisition, including the Holy Office of Malta, as a method of procedure for eliciting declarations of 'truth' from those accused of having committed a 'crime' against the Catholic Faith. The introduction of the use of torture as part of inquisitorial procedure goes back to the bull *Ad Extirpanda* of Pope Innocent IV in 1252, when he allowed its use against the Albigensians, a heretic sect originating in Provence. In using torture, however, the Inquisition was simply living up to contemporary standards. In the case of the Holy Office, in fact, more than a case for the human rights of those under arrest, it was a question of the tribunal's responsibility to save the soul of the accused, at all costs! Until well into the eighteenth century torture was considered an essential

The Tribunal room at the Inquisitor's Palace

The Inquisitor's Palace, Vittoriosa

part of the legal procedure throughout Europe, expounded by a matter-of-course attitude by generations of jurists. The accused was considered the principal means to arrive at the truth, and truth was superior to any bodily pain.[2] Very few voices were raised against its use during the seventeenth century, among which were those of the German Jesuits Adam Tanner and Frederic von Spee.[3] Even the Italian Giovanni Battista Scanaroli defined it as inhuman, absurd, and barbarous.[4] However, torture was an accepted tool in the fact-finding process, an official form of physical injury that reflected a particular attitude towards the body that gave little thought to physical pain or body integrity.[5] In a world and culture where imprisonment was mostly reserved for those awaiting trial, punishment was normally carried out publicly in the form of severe corporal suffering, ranging from execution on the scaffold and mutilation to whipping and branding in order to 'educate' the spectators.[6]

A CAUTIOUS TRIBUNAL

In this respect, the policy of circumspection followed by the Inquisition as regards torture compares favourably with other contemporary secular institutions.[7] Ecclesiastical tribunals could not kill or shed blood, and it has become an established fact that they were certainly not the worst offenders in this field.[8] This applies also for the Spanish Inquisition, which was certainly harsher than the Roman Inquisition as regards torture and applied it much more frequently.[9]

In the very first place it has to be pointed out that contrary to contemporary practice by secular tribunals, torture was not considered to be an end in itself by the Holy Office and was never used as a punishment. Torture was the exception rather than the rule for inquisitorial procedure. In fact, torture was far from being systematically applied, as it was, for instance, in the law courts of secular governments of the time, often basing itself on very flimsy and vague evidence.[10] The duration of torture was also much less than that of secular tribunals, where it was practically without limit. In 1752, for instance, a seventy-year-old man accused of theft from a shop in Valletta was tortured for eighteen hours by the civil courts of the Order of St John.[11]

There was a general reluctance to use torture by the Holy Office. As the Inquisition manuals themselves pointed out, 'Torture is rarely resorted to since experience shows that it does not bear any fruit. In serious cases it is much better if torture is not used at all and the punishment increased instead'.[12] In fact only a very small percentage of cases ever included the

Public humiliation could be defined as another form of turture, even if it was not perceived as such

use of torture. As the councillors of the Holy Office told Inquisitor Ranuccio Pallavicino upon his arrival at the palace in 1676, the Inquisition was itself aware that confessions obtained through torture were not always to be relied upon. Experience had taught them that some of those tortured would be willing to declare or admit anything in order to be relieved from the pain, even that which they never did commit. In 1637, for instance, while undergoing torture, Cesare Pandolfo, accused of bigamy, declared that 'if you want me to tell a lie I will say it, have mercy of me'.[13] Another unfortunate accused said 'I cannot belie myself, but if I do it will be only because of the torments you give me.'[14]

The Holy Office was cautious in applying torture. The inquisitor had to wait first for the go-ahead of his advisory council of consultants and then for a direct permission from his superiors of the Holy Congregation in Rome each time he wanted to use torture. Moreover, torture was rigidly controlled and regulated and had to be applied according to a precise and definite procedure formula. Nor could torture commence if the defence had not yet presented its case. The whole procedure was bureaucratized to the extent that little or nothing was left to the initiative of the inquisitor himself. In fact some inquisitors, such as Fabio Della Lagonessa (1614-19), were even reprimanded for having used torture in cases where it could have easily been avoided.[15]

Opposite: **The notary's desk in the Tribunal Room**

Above: **Some accused were condemned to wear humiliating clothing in public**

TORTURE IN THEORY AND PRACTICE

In theory torture had a threefold aim: to identify the crime, to come to know the crime in detail, and to arrive at the intention with which the crime had been committed.[16] In reality, however, torture was almost always confined to the last of these aims - *super intentione* - as a means to ascertain what intention the accused had in performing his crime, and if he was conscious or not of the consequences of what he was doing. Those tortured, therefore, would be repeatedly asked, for example, if they believed that it was permissible for a Christian to eat meat during Lent, to consult magic healers, or to marry again while the first wife or husband was still alive. They could also be asked if sacraments could be used for any other purpose other than to communicate with God, or if they believed to save their soul if they apostatized to Islam. In other words, torture had to make sure whether the accused had 'misbehaved' because of human frailty in particular circumstances, or if there was a deliberate intellectual refusal (i.e. heresy) of a certain church dogma.

The type of torture used by the Roman Inquisition also had a much lesser element of butchery in it than that of secular courts. Only some of those tortured changed their account as a direct result of that experience; many withstood pain and stuck to their original version of events.[17] In 1635, for instance, Antonia Fontana, a Sicilian living in Valletta, accused of making use of love magic before the Holy Office, denied everything, even under torture.[18] The same

Contrary to the Inquisition, civil tribunals often combined two types of torture at the same time, in this case the *corda* and the *cavalletto* (National Museum of Fine Arts, Inv. No. 15785)

Bollettino da Far et tenir in bocca quando uuol menar qualibet d'usio allto tortura della corda et quando li liga le mani ingiottirlo

Imparibus

Imparibus meriti tria pendenti corpora famis
Dismas egiestas media est Diuina Potestas
Dismas damnatur gestas ad astra leuatur.

A magic formula on how not to feel pain during torture (AIM, Proc. Crim. 97B, case 72, f.670)

happened a century later with Domenico Fregosi who withstood torture without giving in.[19] Some were even strong enough to laugh while being tortured.[20] In such cases the accused would be set free, his case suspended, or else his sentence would be much lighter than if he had admitted his guilt.[21] From this point of view torture was to the advantage of those who had a strong character and who could resist physical pain. Thus, in 1597 the Dominican friar Andrea d'Antora did not receive any sentence at all, since no proof whatsoever was found that he had stolen the chalice of the Dominican church in Valletta, not even under torture.[22] The same occurred to Ignatio la Rocca, who resisted through a torture session in 1703.[23]

However, understandably, contemporary people were terrified by the prospect of being tortured. Some, such as twenty-three-year-old Ignatio Musci from Valletta, in 1703

equipped himself with a magical formula so that he could use it should such an eventuality arise. In order to be able to resist pain, he had to write certain words on a piece of paper, put it into his mouth, and then swallow it as soon as the torture session began.[24] One more extreme case occurred in 1633, when the slave Gio. Batta Cagliares was so terrified of having to face torture that he attempted suicide by eating a fig full of *arsenio e solimato*. However, Giovanni Testaferrata, an official of the Inquisition, realized what Cagliares was trying to do and so forced him to expel the fig from his mouth. The face and lips of Cagliares swelled up but Dr Michele Xeberras, the tribunal's doctor, quickly administered him a *vomitivo* and then *olio di mandole dolci e latte*. His formula evidently left the desired effect since Cagliares recovered so well that he sustained torture and resisted.[25]

TORTURE PROCEDURE

Torture was not applied on those who denounced themselves of their own free will, and it was generally resorted to much more against men rather than against women. Old, weak, disabled, and sick persons or pregnant women were spared the treatment straight away. This was the case of Margarita Curt, a nineteen-year-old prostitute from Valletta. In 1637 she was even dismissed from the prisons of the Holy Office owing to her position by Inquisitor Fabio Chigi and ordered to confine herself to her home instead.[26]

Neither was torture - referred to as *remedia opportuna*[27] - used in cases of petty offences. It was reserved for instances of serious breaches of orthodoxy, when, after a series of interrogations, it was overtly clear that the suspect was lying in the face of evidence, or when there were serious indications that he was refusing to reveal all that he knew.[28] In these cases the accused would be warned that he would be tortured if he still refused to co-operate with the inquisitor. He would then be led to the torture chamber, the *locum tormentos*, as a sort of last warning - *benigne monitus* - to try and convince him to declare everything of his own free will.

Indeed there were even some who were only threatened to be tortured. One such case occurred in 1677, when there was ample proof that Caterina de Riva, a fifty-year-old Maltese prostitute from Valletta, had made use of a series of love magic formulas involving sacramental paraphernalia. But she refused to admit her guilt and was conducted to the torture chamber and shown the torture instruments. She was undressed and examined by the doctor of the Holy Office, Dr Mariano Cassar, as if the torture session was about to start. Yet this type of 'torture', known also as *tortura per territionem*, was only meant to frighten her, as after being questioned for the last time and answering in the same manner, she was led out of the torturing room without being effectively tortured.[29] The same had occurred to Manoli, a thirteen-year-old Greek boy from Crete, accused of apostasy, in 1636.[30] The fact of being threatened with torture and shown the instruments, however, can be considered as a torture in itself.

However if those accused who had been earmarked to be tortured still persisted in their refusal to talk, a doctor and a surgeon would examine them to check if they were healthy enough to withstand torture. In theory those about to be tortured even had the right to refuse a particular torture on medical grounds.[31] However, if the medical examination resulted that the suspect was fit enough for torture, he would take the oath of saying nothing but the truth and be undressed. Only then could the torturer commence with his job, and the doctor would be present during the session to stop the treatment if he was of the opinion that it was beyond the physical resistance of the accused and of clear danger to his health.

Even in the very early years of the tribunal, when the Holy Office was set all out to quash any form of heretical opinion, this procedure was adhered to rigorously. Indeed, in 1574, when Pietro Dusina took over the Inquisitor's Palace as the official seat of the Inquisition, one of his priorities was to have adequate torture

Detailed documentation provide us with impressive and macabre testimonies of the real suffering of the accused

instruments installed in the palace.[32] However, this does not mean that torture was applied indiscriminately. In the same year, in fact, Dr Antonio Tramontana, the medical consultant of the Inquisition, was asked to ascertain whether a man imprisoned by the Holy Office was fit to withstand torture or not. Dr Tramontana certified that the accused had a long history of asthma and suffered from retention of

Figure III

Another method of applying the *corda* (Migliorini, 2001)

Vorstellung des bereits in der Luft aufgewogenen Inquisiten

urine, and therefore he was of the opinion that torture should not be applied in this case.[33] Once more in 1598, Maestro Camillo La Manda, *cirugico del Sant' Officio*, was paid five *scudi* for his services of assisting 'assisting for torture sessions and healing sick prisoners'.[34] This policy never changed throughout the years. In the eighteenth century Pierre Arlò,

a French merchant from Avignon, was spared since the doctor certified that he suffered from asthma and that he could die during torture.[35] This 'human' approach can be contrasted with one extreme case from the Civil Courts of Appeal of the Order of St John. One of the judges, Dr Giulio Cumbo, was notorious for the frequency with which he ordered torture, to the extent that the *cavaletto* was popularly referred to as *il cavallo di Cumbo* (Cumbo's horse). He was also notorious for his readiness to inflict capital punshment with the bonus that the body of the accused had to be quartered and torn apart after execution. When he died aged ninety-six in 1761, he had condemned 120 men to death in forty years.[36]

METHODS OF TORTURE

From the very early decades of the tribunal in Malta, the torture most commonly used (and practically the only one) was the *strappado*, more commonly referred to as *il tormento della corda*. In 1598 the auditor of the Holy Office was instructed to pay 16 *tarì* to Martino Vella, the captain of the rod of the tribunal, 'a rope bought to be used for torture'.[37] In this method the hands of the accused would be tied behind his back, attached to a rope which was thrown over a beam or attached to a pulley or a hook in the ceiling, and the accused would be pulled up in the air. The whole weight of the body would therefore be supported only by the arms and shoulders. He hanged there for a short period of time, then was let down, then raised again. On some occasions when the accused was particularly sturdy, heavy iron weights could be tied to his feet in order to increase the pressure on his arms and

therefore increase the pain.[38] It is indicative to note, however, that while this simple type of torture was used by secular tribunals only as a preliminary warming up to the more refined treatments, it was the main method of torture used by the Inquisition Tribunal. Moreover, the *Diritto Municipale di Malta*, published by in 1784, and considered as enlightened and humanitarian, established that the *strappado* could last for up to one hour at a stretch.[39] In the Holy Office, however, since its setting up in 1542, a torture session could not be applied for longer than half-an-hour. Frequently it took less, generally fifteen minutes, or even less. On one occasion in 1772, for instance, Eugenia Mallia, accused of bigamy, was tortured *per spacius unius minuto*.[40] Time was measured with a sand-clock. Torture, however, could be repeated for two successive days if the accused persisted in his denial.

Above: A half-hour glass clock was used to monitor a torture session

Left: The most common form of torture used by the Roman Inquisition was the *strappado*

This was what Inquisitor Bellardito did to Fra Giulio Pulis, a Dominican friar accused of false oath, in 1587,[41] and what happened to Domenico Fregosi in 1738,[42] while in 1617 Violante Vergotti, accused of dealing in magic, was given the *strappado* on three different occasions.[43]

If the accused had a physical defect, especially in his arms, because of which he could not withstand this kind of torture, he would be applied the next most widely used form of torment, known as the *stanghetta*, or *stringitore*. This was the case of Don Gioseppe and Bartolomeo Haxixa in 1574, who were tortured with the *stanghetta*.[44] Another such instance occurred in 1637, when Valerio Mifsud, a fifty-three-year-old Maltese man from Qormi, was accused of multiple acts of sorcery. In his sentence it was made clear that 'since you are unable to sustain the torture by rope, you were tortured by the *stanghetta*'.[45] This consisted of a leg brace made of two pieces of wood which were pressed on the ankle of the accused.

In some very rare occasions, even the rack, or *cavalletto*, was used. One such case occurred during the tenure of office of Inquisitor Antonio Ortensio (1598-1600) who applied it against Fra Bartolomeo Gattanà, a Dominican friar accused of abusing of sacramental oil, since he was unable to withstand another type of torture.[46] With this method the accused rode over a wooden horse with sharp back. Weights could be attached to the feet. Even Inquisitor Gio. Battista Gori Pannellini (1639-46)

apparently made use of the *cavalletto*.[47] However, it appears that it fell out of use relatively quickly. By 1712 no one of the ministers of the Inquisition remembered it having been used and Inquisitor Raniero d'Elci felt confident enough to affirm that it had never been used by the Holy Office in Malta.[48] By way of contrast, until 1784 those facing the *cavalletto* in the secular courts of Malta could be tortured for up to twelve hours.[49]

The interrogation of the accused during torture was different from the preceding ones during normal court . During the latter, questions were subtle and were generally put in a roundabout way in an attempt to catch the accused in a lie. During torture, however, questions were simple, direct, and to the point. The notary would be present and he had to write down not only the answers of the accused 'even all his arguments and motions and all the words which

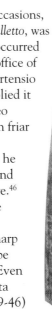

The *cavaletto* (Migliorini, 2001)

14

he proffers during torture, all his sighs, shouts and laments, and all the tears which he sheds',[50] thus providing us with impressive - even if macabre - testimonies of the real (as separated from the fictitious) sufferings of the accused. For instance, in 1637, while undergoing torture, Thomaso Vella, a twenty-eight-year-old cleric from Zurrieq, could not resist the pain any longer and uttered: 'I said the truth. I wish that crucifix could burn me if I did not say the truth, aagh! The broken nerve kills me with pain.'[51]

If the accused admitted his guilt, torture would be immediately stopped, even if the time stipulated for torture had not yet passed. He would have been purified from his sin and was worthy to be re-introduced in the Catholic community. There was no point in continuing further. If he had been given the *strappado*, his arms and shoulders would be put back into their place since they would probably have been dislocated. He would then be re-dressed and helped back into his prison cell - *reportari ad locum suum*. The confession and declaration of guilt had to be confirmed in the courtroom twenty-four hours later, not under torture, in order to become official. If the prisoner recanted, however, the whole procedure could be restarted again.

Above: Typical prison cell furniture: sanitary and sleeping facilities

Left: The *stringitore*

THE TORTURE CHAMBER AND THE TORTURER

Torture always took place behind closed doors in the Inquisitor's Palace and not in public.[52] A plan of the palace of around 1600 shows the torture room located in a distant room with no windows on the first floor in between a store and the servant's room.

According to the inventory of the Inquisitor's Palace of 1631, however, there were two torture chambers, in which there were, among other things, five mattresses and three blankets (for the prisoners), two cupboards, a table, and a bench. The torture instruments (a rope and the *cavalletto*), were kept in the room of prison warden Giuseppe Galdes and taken out for use accordingly.[53] Both torture rooms cannot be traced today because of the great structural

modifications that the palace underwent in subsequent years. Most probably, as the whole palace was practically a building site for long stretches of years, especially the prison complex,[54] the location of the torture chamber would have been changed as circumstances dictated. Presumably it would have simply been transferred to one of the prison cells. By 1676, however, a small cell near the tribunal was used specifically as a torture room and contained a rope attached to a pulley in the ceiling, metal weights, and the *stanghetta*.[55] A torture chamber is mentioned once more in 1700 when, during other major general structural works being carried out in the palace by Inquisitor Giacinto Messerano, a torture room was once more constructed abutting

A communal cell at the Inquisitor's Palace

the tribunal.[56] Possibly this could have been a rehabilitation of the already existing torture room referred to in 1676. In the inventory of the chattels in the palace done by Masserano in 1701, the torture room contained, among other things, the rope with a pulley, the *stringitore*, a stool, and two handcuffs.[57]

It appears that the Holy Office never had a torturer as such employed among its staff. In 1574 Inquisitor Pietro Dusina employed slaves, presumably as an initial temporary measure, to fix the torturing instruments in place and apply torture for the first time.[58] Shortly afterwards it became the policy of the tribunal to make use of officials from the *Magna Curia Castellania* for this purpose. One of the notes of payment of the accountant of the Holy Office in 1598 made reference to 'the secular officials who come to torture and whip the prisoners'.[59] Nor was this an isolated occurrence. The balance sheets of the Holy Office of the second half of the seventeenth century are replete with similar entries. In 1667, for instance, the accountant of the Inquisition recorded the payment of 'Payment of 2 *scudi*, 6 *tari* to officials of the *Castellania* who served the Tribunal to torture and whip the criminals'.[60]

A detail of a *c.* 1600 plan of the Inquisitor's Palace showing the torture chamber marked 'XX', the plan in full is shown on page 30

THE INQUISITORS AND TORTURE

Not all inquisitors adopted the same approach towards torture. Even if its procedure was bureaucratized, its application offered a subjective dimension heavily dependent on the personal character of the inquisitor. Some were harsher than others and sought permission to resort to torture more frequently. This obviously also depended on the type of cases which inquisitors had to decide upon. However, in general, torture was applied more often in the early phases of the tribunal's history.[61] In the first half of the seventeenth century, for instance, Inquisitor Fabio Chigi applied torture on 34 occasions out of the 919 accusations that he had to tackle in the five-year period from 1634 to 1639.[62] This represents a mere 3.7 per cent, but it still was high when compared to later periods. However, even during Chigi's tenure of office, torture was still regarded as an exceptional event, to the extent that he felt the need to note it down in his personal diary.[63]

The use of torture was generally decreasing. In one case in 1653 Don Georgio Gauci, the parish priest of Attard, was heavily suspected of solicitation during confession. It resulted, however, that no conclusive proof could be found against him. Thus, although the cardinal inquisitors of the Holy Congregation were convinced that Don Georgio 'conducted a very loose life not consonant to his position', it was decided that there was not enough proof for him to undergo torture.[64] This attitude became more frequent as time passed. Inquisitor Ercole Visconti did not even resort once to torture during his one-year tenure of office between 1677 and 1678,[65] while the three successive inquisitors, Gio. Antonio Mancinforte (1767-71), Antonio Lante (1771-77), and Antonio Felice Zondadari (1777-85), used torture only once each during the eighteen years in which they held office.[66]

It appears that by the early eighteenth century the use of the *stanghetta* had dwindled to a minimum. In 1687 Ignatio la Roccia, a neophyte slave, was accused of proffering words in favour of Islam. Since he continued to deny this fact in the face of evidence, he was tortured with the *stanghetta*, because he was disabled from one arm and therefore could not be given the *strappado*. He was accused of the same crime in 1703 but he still refused to admit. Inquisitor Giorgio Spinola (1703-06) did not know how to tackle the problem since 'the *stanghetta* is not used in Malta, and although there is this instrument in the Holy Office it has some technical defects, and in any case it rarely bore any fruits'.[67]

Further confirmation of the lack of use of the *stanghetta* occurred in 1718. Inquisitor Lazzaro Pallavicino (1718-19), basing himself on a report presented by the doctor of the tribunal, did not use the *strappado* against Giorgio Mamo, accused of perjury, since it was certified that he could not withstand that kind of treatment. More interesting is the fact that Pallavicino even refused to use the *stanghetta* against him because there was no one of his staff who had ever used this instrument, or knew how to operate it:[68] an indication of how this form of torture had completely fallen out of use. However, it appears that the *stanghetta* became 'popular' once more in the second half

Opposite: **The prison section constructed by Inquisitor Gori Pannellini in the 1640s. The central corridor divided the communal from the solitary cells**

Above: A graffito in one of the prison cells

Opposite: General view of the garden of the Inquisitor's Palace

of torments, torture.[72] In reality, however, inquisitors in general were increasingly contrary to the use of torture. In 1712 Inquisitor Ranieri d'Elci did not approve of this treatment being applied against Filippo Masola who was not able to sustain torture because of his weak physical condition. D'Elci remained of this opinion even though he had received instructions from the Holy Office of Rome to proceed with torture and even if Masola had a very bad character and refused to co-operate in any way with the inquisitor.[73]

The extent to which the use of torture in general had diminished is also demonstrated by the fact that in 1745 Inquisitor Paolo Passionei (1743-54) had to ask the *fiscale* of the *Magna Curia Castellania* if he could provide him not only with the services of the torturer of the civil courts, as was always customary, but also with the torture instrument (the rope) for the *strappado*, because the Holy Office did not even possess one.[74]

It is evident that by the mid-eighteenth century torture had practically fallen out of use. During the last fifty-five years of the tribunal's existence in Malta, between 1743 and 1798, torture was only resorted to on 24 occasions, approximately once every two years. When compared to the total number of denunciations, 3,620, this represents a microscopic 0.6 per cent. The last two inquisitors to hold office in Malta Gio. Filippo Gallarati Scotti (1785-93), and Giulio Carpegna (1793-98) never tortured anyone.[75] The use of torture was finally banned in Roman Catholic countries through an edict issued by Pope Pius VII in1816.

of the eighteenth century since it was used on eight occasions during the fifty-five year period from 1743 to 1798.[69]

As the eighteenth century moved forward, the use of torture came increasingly under attack. A variety of social forces brought about a culture change which developed a marked tendency towards non-physical discipline. This movement reflected changing attitudes towards the human body as a result of a growing sensitivity to violence and an aversion to physical suffering.[70] Consequently, torture was abolished in Prussia in 1754, in Saxony in 1770, and in Poland and Austria in 1776.[71] However, despite the increasing popularity of Enlightenment thought, and the well-known attacks on the use of torture in criminal cases, (such as those of Cesare Beccaria and Voltaire), torture survived well into the eighteenth century in many European States. Criminal procedure had no real alternative to it. The law of proof was absolutely dependent on coerced confessions, and the queen of proofs, confession, required the queen

CONCLUSION

The procedure used by the Inquisition to obtain information, especially secrecy and, most of all, the use of torture, left an indelible mark on the tribunal and on its history. The Holy Office was dreaded and feared – not without reason – by contemporaries as well as by modern-day people. In reality the Inquisition was feared so much because all those who had experienced it were obliged to swear that they could not reveal anything which they had seen or underwent in the Inquisitor's Palace. Although this vow was not always respected, it was perhaps the main reason why so many myths and legends about the palace and what used to take place in it cropped up in the popular imagination and developed later on after the tribunal's suppression. The most famous is without any doubt the notorious 'knife-pit' (*bir tas-skieken*), in which prisoners of the Inquisition were allegedly thrown to their death. Even if such rumours were already circulating in the early modern period,[76] this claim has no documentary or archaeological evidence whatsoever. Rumours increased during the nineteenth century, when both George Badger and William Tallack reported the alleged find of torture instruments in the basement by British soldiers while digging for a wine-cellar in the 1820s.[77]

What was thought to be the infamous knife pit was excavated by Vincenzo Bonello, the curator of the Fine Arts Section of the Museums Department, in 1927-28, and it turned out to be a very normal and simple 'bell-shaped well eight feet six inches deep',[78] the like of which there are at least another twelve in the Inquisitor's Palace.

However, once similar stories get entrenched in popular mentality they are practically impossible to eradicate. Thus in 1966 Robin Bryans, in his guide to Malta and Gozo, made reference to the 'well of knives' in the palace.[79] The actual existence of such stories became so deep-rooted that sometimes they are taken for granted still. Nor did the Church authorities help in eradicating these legends either. The fact that the archives of the Inquisition were made available to researchers only in the late 1960s, presumably because of fears that these rumours might be proved correct, simply added fuel to the flames. However, this aura of secrecy was perhaps the most effective way to engender fear of the Inquisition and its activities and to induce people to conform to Church teachings and denounce others who did not, at least outwardly. If this was not done not out of personal conviction, action was taken because of fear of what could happen if he or she was discovered – a fear more imaginary than real, especially by contemporary standards of human rights. This procedure ensured the eventual success of the Inquisition and the indelible mark it left on society: in the time of the Inquisition it was dangerous either to speak or to be silent; up to this day Maltese people tend to speak in one way and think in another.

Opposite: The cess-pit of one of the prison cells

EXAMPLE OF A TORTURE SESSION

Interrogation of Cesare Pandolfo, a thirty-six-year-old Italian sailor from Naples living in Vittoriosa, accused of bigamy, on whether it was permissible for a Christian to marry again while his first wife was still alive and on how he induced witnesses to testify that he had not been married before.[80]

Die xxvi mensis Febrarii 1637

Coram Illustrissimo Domino Inquisitore et assistente Dom. Assessore et Dom. Fisci promotore.

Eductus e carceribi et personali constitutus iteru supradicto Cesar Pandolfus cui delato iuramento de veritate dicenda tactis sacris scripturis.

Interrogatus iteru, et benigne monitus ut dicat veritate au vere credat vel crediderit licere catholico havere eodem tempore duas uxores.

Respondit: Io so benissimo che non è lecito haver due mogli in un medesimo tempo, e non ho creduto mai, ne credo che si possino havere due mogli insieme.

Et sibi dicto misi se resolvat fateri ulteriorem veritatem et credulitatem super premissis opus erit con eum devenire ad Iuris et facti remedia opportuna p ut devenietur ad tortura.

Respondit: Io gia ho detto la verità che li testimoni supponendo alle semplici parole del quondam Dottor Camenzuli, e mie che io fossi schetto, hanno deposto in mio favore, et io non credo ne ho creduto mai esser lecito al cristiano d'haver due mogli in un medesimo tempo.

Tunc Illustrissimus Dominus adherendo suptio Decreto Congregationis mandavit … conventu duci ad locum tormentos et ibi spoliari visitari ligari et funi applicari, et … opus torqueri pro habenda ulteriori veritate, et intentione, citra … cum fisci … Iuriu p.bator et confessatorum et non aliter nec alio modo sic istante, et petente huius Sancti Officii Promotore fiscali

Qui sic ad locu tormentos adductus et spoliatus fuit visitatus p maestrum Thomam Sapiano chirurgus huius Sancto

The fourteenth day of February 1637

In the presence of His Eminence the Inquisitor [Fabio Chigi] with the assistance of the assessor and the fiscal procurator [public prosecutor]. The above-mentioned Cesare Pandolfo was escorted out of his prison cell and presented. He touched the Holy Scriptures and took the oath of saying the truth.

He was questioned and warned benignly to say the truth if he really believed that it was licit for a Catholic to marry two women at the same time.

He answered: 'I know perfectly well that it is not allowed to have two women at the same time, and I never believed, nor do I believe, that it is permitted to marry two women contemporaneously.'

After his answer he was once more warned that, if he does not say the truth about his beliefs on the above question, it would be necessary to use the required means (torture) so that he would declare the truth.

He replied: 'I have already said the truth. The witnesses believed the words of the late Dr Camenzuli and mine that I was not married and deposed in my favour. I do not believe and never believed that a Christian can marry two women at the same time.'

The inquisitor having heard this answer, following the instructions received from the Holy Congregation, ordered that Pandolfo be taken to the torture room to be undressed, visited by the doctor, and tied to the rope so that he would declare and confess all

Officio qui medio eius iuramento dixit ipsu constitutum esse ad tortura sustinenda aptu.

Et tunc d. constitutus dum ligaretur fuit benigne monitus et hortatus ut tandem veritatem dicat supra quesitis ad eo et recedat ab eius pertinacia nec expectet … in funem elevatur.

Respondit: Io gia ho detto la verità come i testimoni hanno deposto à mio favore, et io non ho mai creduto esser lecito haver due mogli in un medesimo tempo.

Et ligatus et funi

applicatus p
Oliviero Seychel cursorem huius Sancti Officii qui retulit eu benigne ligasse medio eius iuramento.

… elevatur fuit iteru benigne monitus ad … veritatem et modu quo induxit testes ad deponendu in sui favorem, et au credat, vel crediderit cristiano cattolico licere duas uxores eodem tempore habere.

Respondit: Io gia ho detto di non credere che il cristiano possa havere due mogli insieme, et io ho detto anco in che

the truth about his intentions in the presence of the public prosecutor and the assessor and in no other way.

Pandolfo was therefore conducted to the torture chamber, undressed, and visited by the surgeon of the Holy Office Dr Thomas Sapiano who, after taking an oath, declared that the accused was fit to sustain torture.

After being conducted to the torture room and tied to the rope, he was once again warned and exhorted so that finally he would declare the whole truth on the above question, and that by repeating the same answer he would have to be pulled up in the air.

He replied: 'I have already said the truth as the witnesses deposed in my favour. I have never believed that it was allowed to have two wives at the same time.'

He was therefore tied to the rope by Oliviero Seychel, cursor of the Hoy Office, who declared under oath that Pandolfo had been tied well.

Before being raised, he was kindly warned to say the truth how he had induced the witnesses to depose in his favour, and if he believes or believed it was licit for a Catholic to marry two women at the same time.

He replied: 'I have already said that I do not believe that a Christian can have two wives at the same time, and I have also said how the witnesses deposed.'

Having heard this answer, the Inquisitor ordered that he be raised from the ground. Once he was in the air he started to shout, saying 'Oh Virgin Mary help me, I am dying.' He was once more benevolently warned

An inquisition's sentence of the 1630s

modo i testimoni hanno deposto.

Tunc Illustrissimus Dominus mandavit illu in altu elevari. Qui si elevatus, cepit clamare dicendo ò Maria Vergine aiutatemi io son morto. Et benigne monitus ad ... veritatem circa modo quo induxit testes et credulitatem.

Respondit: Io gia ho detto quel che dovevo dire, la Madonna del Rosario m'aiuti.

Et iteru monitus ut dicat veritatem circa premissa.

Respondit: Non ho che dire più di quel che ho detto e non mi fate morire, continuo clamando oyme oyme che moro.

Et monitus ut recedat ab eius pertinacia et dicat veritatem circa premissa.

Respondit: Io ho detto la verità vociferando oyme oyme; per l'amor di Dio non saccio che dire più.

Et iteru interrogatu de veritate circa premissa.

Respondit: se volete che io dichi la bugia lo dirrò, ma la verità e come ho detto, mi tormentate, et io non ho che dire oltre di quello ho detto, et habbiate misericordia di me.

Et ... alium ab eo haberi non possit, ... in tormentis sia elevatus stetisset per quadrantem mandatu fuit illu leviter deponi solui, bracchia aptari, revestiri, et in locum suum reduci ... p ut fuit depositus, solutus, brachia aptata, revestitus, et in locum suum repositus.

to declare the truth on how he had induced the witnesses and on his beliefs.

He answered: 'I have already said what I had to say, may Our Lady of the Rosary help me.'

He was once more asked to say the truth.

He replied: 'I have nothing more to say than what I have already said, do not kill me.' He continued to shout aagh, aagh I am dying.'

He was once again asked not to remain obstinate and declare the truth.

He replied: 'I have already said the truth,' shouting 'aagh, aagh, for the love of God I do not know what else to say.'

He was again questioned on the above.

He replied: 'If you want me to tell a lie I will, but the truth is what I have already said. You torture me but I do not have anything else to say more than I have already said, have mercy on me.'

Seeing that he could not resist any more, having been tortured for a quarter of an hour, the inquisitor ordered that he be lowered to the ground, his shoulders put in place, re-dressed, and conducted back to his prison cell. He was therefore lowered, his shoulders were put in place, and he was re-dressed and escorted to the prison cell.

INQUISITORS OF MALTA 1562-1798

Domenico Cubelles (Bishop of Malta 1541-66)	1562-1566
Martino Royas de Portalrubeo (Bishop of Malta 1566-77)	1572-1574
Pietro Dusina	1574-1575
Pietro Sant'Umano	1575-1577
Rinaldo Corso	1577-1579
Domenico Petrucci	1579-1580
Federico Cefalotto	1580-1583
Pietro Francesco Costa	1583-1585
Ascanio Libertano	1585-1587
Giovanni Battista Petralata	1587
Paolo Bellardito	1587-1591
Angelo Gemmario	1591
Paolo Bellardito	1591-1592
Giovanni Ludovico dell'Armi	1592-1595
Innocenzo del Bufalo de'Cancellieri	1595-1598
Antonio Hortensio	1598-1600
Fabrizio Verallo	1600-1605
Ettore Diotallevi	1605-1607
Leonetto della Corbara	1607-1608
Evangelista Carbonese	1608-1614
Fabio della Lagonessa	1614-1619
Antonio Tornielli	1619-1621
Paolo Torello	1621-1623
Carlo Bovio	1623-1624
Onorato Visconti	1624-1627
Nicolò Herrera	1627-1630
Ludovico Serristori	1630-1631
Martino Alfieri	1631-1634
Fabio Chigi (Pope Alexander VII 1655-67)	1634-1639
Giovanni Battista Gori Pannellini	1639-1646
Antonio Pignatelli (Pope Innocent XII 1691-1700)	1646-1649
Carlo Cavalletti	1649-1652
Federico Borromeo	1653-1654
Giulio degli Oddi	1655-1658
Gerolamo Casanate	1658-1663
Galeazzo Marescotti	1663-1666
Angelo Ranuzzi	1667-1668
Carlo Bichi	1668-1670
Giovanni Tempi	1670-1672
Ranuccio Pallavicino	1672-1676
Ercole Visconti	1677-1678
Giacomo Cantelmo	1678-1683
Innico Caracciolo	1683-1686
Tommaso Vidoni	1686-1690
Francesco Aquaviva d'Aragona	1691-1694
Tommaso Ruffo	1694-1698

Frescoes of the coat-of-arms of some of Inquisitors in the main hall of the *piano nobile*, the one (third from left) with the papal tiare indicates that the inquisitor subsequently became pope, Alexander VII

Giacinto Filiberto di Messerano	1698-1703
Giorgio Spinola	1703-1706
Giacomo Caracciolo	1706-1710
Ranieri d'Elci	1711-1715
Lazzaro Pallavicino	1718-1719
Antonio Ruffo	1720-1728
Fabrizio Serbelloni	1728-1730
Giovanni Francesco Stoppani	1731-1735
Carlo Francesco Durini	1735-1739
Ludovico Gualtiero Gualtieri	1739-1743
Paolo Passionei	1743-1754
Gregorio Salviati	1754-1759
Angelo Maria Durini	1760-1766
Giovanni Antonio Mancinforte	1767-1771
Antonio Lante	1771-1777
Antonio Felice Zondadari	1777-1785
Giovanni Filippo Gallarati Scotti	1785-1793
Giulio Carpegna	1793-1798

NOTES

1 E. Peters, 'Prison before the prison', in *The Oxford history of the prison. The practice of punishment in western society*, N. Morris and D. J. Rothman (ed.), (Oxford, 1985), 31.

2 C. Fornili, *Delinquenti e carcerati a Roma alla meta del '600* (Rome, 1991), 168; S. Derom, *Museum of torture instruments* (Gent, 1995), 16.

3 D. Sella, *L'Italia del Seicento* (Rome-Bari, 2000), 316.

4 Fornili, 130

5 P. Spierenburg, 'The body and the state. Early modern Europe', in *The Oxford history of the prison*, 49-50.

6 See P. Spierenburg, *The spectacle of suffering. Executions and the evolution of repression from a preindustrial metropolis to the European experience* (Cambridge, 1994).

7 M. Weisser, 'Crime and punishment in early modern Spain', in *Crime and the law. The social history of crime in western Europe since 1500*, V.A.C. Gatrell, B. Lenman and G. Parker (eds), (London, 1980), 81.

8 See G. Neilson, 'Torture', in *Encyclopedia of religion and ethics*, ed. J. Hastings, XII (Edinburgh, 1921), 393.

9 H. Kamen, *The Spanish Inquisition. An historical revision* (London, 1998), 187-92. See also G. Riley Scott, *Storia della tortura*, trans. S. Bigliazzi (Milan, 1999), 86-107.

10 See M. Foucault, *Discipline and punish. The birth of the prison*, trans. A. Sheridan (Harmondsworth, 1979); E. Peters, *Torture* (Oxford, 1985); P. Verri, *Osservazioni sulla tortura*, ed. F. Cuomo (Rome, 1994).

11 A. Bonnici, *Storja ta' l-Inkizizzjoni ta' Malta*, III (Malta, 1994), 177.

12 A[rchives of the] I[nquisition of] Malta, Misc[ellanea].2, *Pratica per procedere nelle cause del Sant' Officio*, 78.

13 AIM, Proc[essi] Crim[inali].52A, case 172, ff. 195v-7.

14 F. Ciappara, *Society and the Inquisition in early modern Malta* (Malta, 2001), 437.

15 A. Bonnici, *Medieval and Roman Inquisition in Malta* (Malta, 1998), 166.

16 I. Mereu, *Storia dell' intolleranza in Europa* (Milan, 1995), 217.

17 J. Tedeschi, *Il giudice e l'eretico. Studi sull'Inquisizione Romana* (Milan, 1997), 113.

18 AIM, Proc. Crim.51A, case 18, f. 66v.

19 AIM, Corr[ispondenza].95, f. 64v, Durini to Holy Congregation, 28 July 1738.

20 Ciappara, 437.

21 See J. Langbein, *Torture and the law of proof.*

22 M. Fsadni, *Id-Dumnikani fir-Rabat u l-Birgu sa l-1620* (Malta, 1974), 232.

23 AIM, Corr.94, f. 71v, Spinola to Holy Congregation, 8 July 1703.

24 Ibid., Proc. Crim.97B, case 72, ff. 670-1. Other similar instances are quoted by Ciappara, 436.

25 Ibid., 50A, case 185, ff. 248-51: 'purgative substance ... walnut oil and milk'.

26 Ibid., 51A, case 82, f. 400v.

27 Ibid., 55B, case 237, f. 812.

28 See J. Tedeschi, 'Inquisitorial law and the witch', in *Early modern European witchcraft. Centres and peripheries*, B. Ankarloo and G. Henningsen (ed.), (Oxford, 1990), 97-8.

29 AIM, Proc. Crim.79, case 1, ff. 108-v. 18 August 1677.

30 Ibid., 51B, case 167, ff. 1052-6.

31 T. Menghini, *Sacro arsenale, ovvero pratica dell'uffizio della Santa Inquisizione* (Ferrara, 1687), 250, as quoted by A. Migliorini, *Tortura, Inquisizione, pena di morte* (Siena, 2001), 38.

32 AIM, Proc. Crim., Prae IB, ff. 37v-38.

33 Fsadni, 80-86.

34 AIM, Conti. Computa Sant' Officio 1598-1600, unpaginated loose papers.

35 Ciappara, 442.

36 P. Cassar, 32-33

37 AIM, Conti, unpaginated loose papers. .

38 A. Bonnici, 'Inkwizitur li, fi xjuhitu, jhewden fuq zmienu f'Malta', *Il-Mument*, 19 May 2002, 20.

39 D. Borg-Muscat, 'Prison life in Malta in the 18th century. Valletta's Gran Prigione', *Storja 2001* (Malta, 2001), 48.

40 AIM, Proc. Crim.130, case 37, f. 456.

41 Fsadni, 221.

42 Ciappara, 438.

43 C. Cassar, *Sex, magic and the periwinkle. A trial at the Malta Inquisition tribunal* (Malta, 2000), 25-7.

44 AIM, Proc. Crim., Prae IB, f. 38.

45 Ibid., 44B, case 100, f. 1055.

46 Fsadni, 234-5.

47 A. Bonnici, 'The use of torture', *Civilization*, I, 469.

48 AIM, Corr.94, f. 182, d'Elci to Holy Congregation, 12 November 1712.

49 Borg-Muscat, 49.

50 E. Masini, *Arsenale ovvero prattica della*

Santa Inquisitione (Genoa, 1621). As quoted in Mereu, 215.

51 AIM, Proc. Crim.51A, case 82, f. 420.

52 Ibid., Corr.1, f. 241v, Cardinal Arigoni to Diotallei, 20 May 1606: 'La tortura si dia nelli carceri del Sant' Officio … nel luogo ove il reo processato si trovarà ritenuto'.

53 AIM, Proc. Civ., Inventario 1631, ff. 269-71v.

54 See K. Gambin, *The prison experience at the Inquisitor's Palace* (Malta, 2002).

55 Bonnici, 'Inkwizitur', 20.

56 A. Bonnici, 238

57 AIM, Corr.94, f. 27, Messerano to Cardinal Cybo, 13 February 1700.

58 Ibid., Proc. Crim., Prae IB, f. 37v: 'Per dar la corda la prima volta alli schiavi … quando si volse frustar le due donne'.

59 Ibid., Conti. Computa Sant' Officio 1598-1601, unpaginated loose papers.

60 AIM, Computa 1658-1709, f. 41v.

61 See G. Lauri, 'Crime and punishment in the court of the Inquisition 1600-1640', *Archivum. The journal of Maltese historical research*, 1 (1981), 44-64.

62 K. Gambin, 'Fabio Chigi: Inquisitor-Missionary and Tridentine Reformer' (Unpublished MA dissertation, University of Malta, 1997), 47.

63 B[iblioteca] A[postolica] V[aticana], [Archivio] Chigi, a.I.8(4), f. 58v, 14 August 1635, 'si da la corda'.

64 AIM, Proc. Crim.68B, case 69, f. 555.

65 K. Gambin, 'Popular culture and the Inquisition 1677-1678', (Unpublished B.A. Hons dissertation, University of Malta, 1995).

66 Ciappara, 436.

67 AIM, Corr.94, ff. 67v-68, Spinola to Marescotti, 24 March 1703.

68 Ibid., ff. 213v-214, Pallavicino to Holy Congregation, 25 June 1718. See Bonnici, *Storja ta' l-Inkizizzjoni ta' Malta*, II (Malta, 1992), 367-8.

68 Ciappara, 439.

69 See P. Spierenburg, *Prison experience. Disciplinary institutions and their inmates in early modern Europe* (Rutgers Univ. Press, 1991).

70 B. Lenman and G. Parker, 'The State, the community and the criminal law in early modern Europe', in V.A.C. Gattrell, B. Lenman and G. Parker (ed.), *Crime and the law*, 42.

71 Peters, *Torture*, 69-72.

72 AIM, Corr.94, f. 182, D'Elci to Holy Congregation, 12 November 1712. See Bonnici, II, 355.

73 N[ational] L[ibrary of] M[alta], Lib[rary]. 638, unpaginated, 13 October 1745.

74 Ciappara, 66, 436-9.

75 Ibid., 444.

76 G. P. Badger, *Description of Malta and Gozo* (Malta, 1838), 213; W. Tallack, *Malta under the Phenicians, Knights and English* (London, 1861), 84.

78 *Museum Annual Report 1927-28*, p.xviii.

79 R. Bryans, *Malta and Gozo* (London, 1966), 148.

80 AIM, Proc. Crim.52A, case 172, ff. 185v-7.

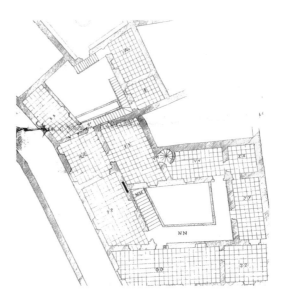

A plan of the first floor of the Inquisitor's Palace of *c.* 1600

BIBLIOGRAPHY

Primary Manuscript Sources

Archives of the Inquisition of Malta
    AIM, Proc. Crim. Prae IB, *Registrum introitus et exitus Sanct. Inquisitionis 1563-1635*
    AIM, Proc. Crim. 44B
    AIM, Proc. Crim. 50A
    AIM, Proc. Crim. 51A
    AIM, Proc. Crim. 51B
    AIM, Proc. Crim. 52A
    AIM, Proc. Crim. 55B
    AIM, Proc. Crim. 68B
    AIM, Proc. Crim. 79
    AIM, Proc. Crim. 97B
    AIM, Proc. Crim. 130
    AIM, Corr. 1
    AIM, Corr. 94
    AIM, Corr. 95
    AIM, Conti. Computa Sant' Officio 1598-1600
    AIM, Computa 1658-1709
    AIM, Misc.2, *Pratica per procedere nelle cause del Sant' Officio.*
    AIM, Proc. Civ., *Inventario 1631*

National Library of Malta
    Lib. 638

Biblioteca Apostolica Vaticana
    Archivio Chigi, a.I.8(4)

Secondary Printed Sources

Badger, G. P., *Description of Malta and Gozo* (Malta, 1838).
Bennassar, B., *Storia dell'Inquisizione spagnola* (Milan, 1995).
Bonnici, A., 'Inkwizitur li, fi xjuħitu, jhewden fuq żmienu f'Malta', *Il-Mument*, 19 May 2002, 20.
Bonnici, A., 'The use of torture', *Civilization*, I.
Bonnici, A., *Medieval and Roman Inquisition in Malta* (Malta, 1998).
Bonnici, A., *Storja ta' l-Inkiżizzjoni ta' Malta*, II-III (Malta, 1992-94).
Bonnici, A., 'Malta dai manoscritti della Stanza storica dell'Archivio della Congregazione della Fede', *Melita Historica*, XIII, 3 (2002), 229-38
Borg-Muscat, D., 'Prison life in Malta in the 18th century. Valletta's *Gran Prigione*', *Storja 2001* (Malta, 2001).
Bryans, R., *Malta and Gozo* (London, 1966).
Cassar, C., *Sex, magic, and the periwinkle. A trial at the Malta Inquisition tribunal* (Malta, 2000).
Cassar, P., *The Castellania Palace: from Law Courts to guardian of the nation's health* (Malta, 1988)
Ciappara, F., *Society and the Inquisition in early modern Malta* (Malta, 2001).
Derom, S., *Museum of torture instruments* (Gent, 1995).
Fornili, C., *Delinquenti e carcerati a Roma alla meta del '600* (Rome, 1991).

Foucault, M., *Discipline and punish. The birth of the prison*, trans. A. Sheridan (Harmondsworth, 1979).

Fsadni, M., *Id-Dumnikani fir-Rabat u l-Birgu sa l-1620* (Malta, 1974).

Gambin, K., 'Fabio Chigi: Inquisitor-Missionary and Tridentine Reformer' (Unpublished MA dissertation, University of Malta, 1997).

Gambin, K., 'Popular culture and the Inquisition 1677-1678', (Unpublished BA Hons dissertation, University of Malta, 1995).

Gambin, K., *The prison experience at the Inquisitor's Palace* (Malta, 2002).

Gatrell, V.A.C., Lenman, B., and Parker, G. (eds), *Crime and the law. The social history of crime in western Europe since 1500* (London, 1980).

Hastings, J., (ed.), *Encyclopedia of religion and ethics*, XII (Edinburgh, 1921).

Kamen, H., *The Spanish Inquisition. An historical revision* (London, 1998).

Langbein, J., *Torture and the law of proof. Europe and England in the Ancien Regime* (Chicago, 1976).

Lauri, G., 'Crime and punishment in the court of the Inquisition 1600-1640', *Archivum. The journal of Maltese historical research*, 1 (1981), 44-64.

Lenman, B., and Parker, G., 'The State, the community and the criminal law in early modern Europe', in Gattrell, Lenman and Parker (eds), *Crime and the law* (London, 1980).

Masini, E., *Arsenale ovvero prattica della Santa Inquisitione* (Genoa, 1621).

Menghini T., *Sacro arsenale, ovvero pratica dell'uffizio della Santa Inquisizione* (Ferrara, 1687).

Mereu, I., *Storia dell' intolleranza in Europa* (Milan, 1995).

Migliorini, A., *Tortura, Inquisizione, pena di morte* (Siena, 2001).

Morris, N., and Rothman, D. J., (eds.), *The Oxford history of the prison. The practice of punishment in western society* (Oxford, 1985).

Museum Annual Report 1927-28.

Neilson, G., 'Torture', in *Encyclopedia of religion and ethics*, ed. J. Hastings, XII (Edinburgh, 1921).

Peters, E., 'Prison before the prison', in *The Oxford history of the prison. The practice of punishment in western society*, N. Morris and D. J. Rothman (eds.), (Oxford, 1985).

Peters, E., *Torture* (Oxford, 1985).

Riley Scott, G., *Storia della tortura*, trans. S. Bigliazzi (Milan, 1999).

Sella, D., *L'Italia del Seicento* (Rome-Bari, 2000).

Spierenburg, P., 'The body and the state. Early modern Europe', in *The Oxford history of the prison. The practice of punishment in western society*, N. Morris and D. J. Rothman (eds.), (Oxford, 1985).

Spierenburg, P., *Prison experience. Disciplinary institutions and their inmates in early modern Europe* (Rutgers Univ. Press, 1991).

Spierenburg, P., *The spectacle of suffering. Executions and the evolution of repression from a preindustrial metropolis to the European experience* (Cambridge, 1994).

Tallack, W., *Malta under the Phenicians, Knights and English* (London, 1861).

Tedeschi, J., 'Inquisitorial law and the witch', in *Early modern European witchcraft. Centres and peripheries*, B. Ankarloo and G. Henningsen (ed.), (Oxford, 1990).

Tedeschi, J., *Il giudice e l'eretico. Studi sull'Inquisizione Romana* (Milan, 1997).

Verri, P., *Osservazioni sulla tortura*, ed. F. Cuomo (Rome, 1994).

Weisser, M., 'Crime and punishment in early modern Spain', in *Crime and the law. The social history of crime in western Europe since 1500*, V.A.C. Gatrell, B. Lenman and G. Parker (eds), (London, 1980).